Preach & Pray

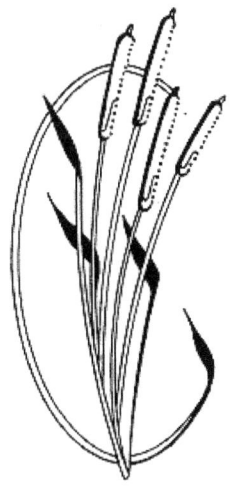

"HE DID IT!"

Preach & Pray

Nadine V. Hadley

Senior Publisher
Steven Lawrence Hill Sr

ASA Publishing Corporation

A Publisher Trademark Title page

ASA Publishing Corporation
An Accredited Publishing House with the BBB
www.asapublishingcorporation.com

The Landmark Building
23 E. Front St., Suite 103, Monroe, Michigan 48161

All Rights Reserved. No part of this publication may be reproduced, stored in a retrieval system or transmitted in any form or by any means electronic, mechanical, photocopying, recording or otherwise, without the prior written permission of the publisher. Author/writer rights to "Freedom of Speech" protected by and with the "1st Amendment" of the Constitution of the United States of America. This is a work of non-fiction; religious freedom of prayer and worship. Any resemblance to actual events, locales, person living or deceased that is not related to the author's literacy is entirely coincidental.

With this title/copyrights page, the reader is notified that the publisher does not assume, and expressly disclaims any obligation to the authors own workings, within the author's rights as manuscript owner. Nor is the publisher obligated to obtain and/or include any other information other than that provided by the author (unless permitted) and within the ownership rights thereof. Any belief system, promotional motivations, including but not limited to the use of non-fictional/fictional characters and/or characteristics of this book, are within the boundaries of the author's own creativity in order to reflect the nature and concept of the book.

Any and all vending sales and distribution not permitted without full book cover and this copyrights page.

Copyrights
©2017 Nadine V. Hadley, All Rights Reserved
Book Title: Preach & Pray
Date Published: 10.02.2017 / Edition 1 *Trade Paperback*
Book ID: ASAPCID2380737
ISBN: 978-1-946746-20-7
Library of Congress Cataloging-in-Publication Data

This book was published in the United States of America
Great State of Michigan

A Publisher Trademark Copyrights page

-Dedication-

In writing this Book it is totally instructed by God. You don't know how many lives you can help by just following the guidance of the Holy Spirit. You can help so many people when they hear a Sermon. Sometimes people say: "You're preaching to me," Or "How do They know about my Life." So Dig in, Sit Back and let your mind and your heart see what the Lord has to say. Amen!

Author

This Book is written from the NKJV. It is for your understanding to make it easy to explain the message God wants to use for such a time as this. Pray, Receive, Comprehend, and Believe on Jesus Christ to bring you through anything that man can not. Who could have thought by the Word mix Faith we are saved from a burning Hell.

There is Something about the Word of God Being spirit, life, power and strength which brings us into completeness. It's the Bible, the bestselling book on the market. There is none to compare with it. All knowing, all seeing ancient of days.

The only thing God is angry with is Sin and doubt in him. Not the Sinner, because we were born in Sin Shaped in iniquity. I don't know about you but I'm just going to trust and believe God and his Word.

I just have a few people I want to Thank. Most of all I Thank my Heavenly Father my Lord Jesus Christ for this opportunity to give me knowledge to write this on paper. Thank you Jesus!!!! Then I want to Thank My Pastor Lewis Savage and First Lady Norma Savage for teaching me the Word of God for the last 20 years. Growing me up to be the Spiritual Woman I am today. I want to Thank Bryant Rogers telling me to stay on task with my messages. Joyce Vidales sending me Scriptures everyday for the last few years. And Elder Jackie Ellis my weekend Prayer Warrior, Tammy Desembly another praying partner. But I can never forget my back up and friend and Sister that proof read this book Mary McDonald. Ms. Mary is my Sister in the Lord and best friend. THANK YOU ALL ONCE AGAIN!!!!!!

Table of Contents

WHAT TIME IS IT? 1
LORD YOU ARE GOOD 6
GOOD MORNING LORD 8
THE GREAT PHYSICIAN 10
REPENT AND PROSPER 11
DON'T LOSE YOUR SONG 16
YOU REAP WHAT YOU SOW 19
LABOR OF LOVE PRAYER 23
I'M CHOSEN 24
HELL WAS NOT MADE FOR YOU 29
MY PRAYERS MAKES A DIFFERENCE 34
PRAYERS CHANGES THINGS 36
VIRTUOUS 42
FROM THE CURSE TO GRACE 49
YOUR FAITH MAKES YOU PRAISE 54
SOME ONE'S KNOCKING AT THE DOOR 59
IT CAME FROM YOUR WOMB 64
IT'S PRAYING TIME 69
WHAT ARE YOU DOING WITH YOUR TIME? (SEEK HIM) . 73
THERE IS A FINALLY 77
I MADE IT 81

Preach & Pray

Nadine V. Hadley

WHAT TIME IS IT?

Eccl. 3: v2 v8

² A time to be born

And a time to die

A time to plant

And a time to pluck up what is planted.

⁸ A time to love

And time to hate

A time of war

And a time of peace

You may been born in March, or June, January, November even April, But that's not good enough.

With God. You must be born again! You asked a question what does that mean? Well I'm glad you asked. Have you been quickened with the Spirit. I'm talking about the Holy Spirit. The Spirit that will give you everlasting life with Jesus. Make you love thee unlovable. Make you forgive someone who mistreated you even when they were in the wrong.

John 3:2,3

Talks about a man name Nicodemus a ruler of the Jews.

> ² This man came to Jesus by night and said to him Rabbi, we know that You are a teacher came from God for no one can do these signs that you do unless God is with him . . .
>
> ³ Jesus answered and said to him, "Most Assuredly, I say to you unless one is born again, he cannot see the kingdom of God."

What time is it?

> It's time for One to Plant, One to Water, But God gives the Increase.
>
> Luke 13:6-9
>
> ⁶ He also spoke this parable: "A certain man had a fig tree planted in his vineyard, and he came seeking fruit on it and found none.
>
> ⁷ Then he said to the keeper of his vineyard, "Look, for three years I have come seeking

fruit on this fig tree and find none. Cut it down; why does it use up the ground?

⁸ But he answered and said to him, 'Sir let it alone this year also until I dig around it and fertilize it.

⁹ And if it bears fruit, well. But if not, after that you can cut it down,"

What time is it?

Since Someone planted the Word in your heart. Don't harden your heart, don't shut God out. There will come a time when you call on God and he will laugh at your calamity.

What time is it?

It's time to love your brothers and sisters unconditionally. Love works no evil to his neighbor. It's to your credit to overlook a transgression.

1 Corinthians 13:4-8a

⁴ Love suffers long and is kind, Loves does not envy, love does not parade itself, is not puff up;

⁵ does not behave rudely does not seek its own, is not provoked, thinks no evil;

> [6] Does not rejoice in iniquity, but rejoices in the truth
>
> [7] bears all things, believes all things, hopes all things endures all things.
>
> [8a] Love never fails.

What time is it?

It's time to love what God loves and hate what God hates.

Proverbs 6:16-19

> [16] These six things the Lord hates, Yes, seven are an abomination to Him:
>
> [17] A proud look, A lying tongue, Hand s that shed innocent blood,
>
> [18] A heart that devises wicked plans, Feet that are swift in running to evil,
>
> [19] A false witness who speaks lies, And one who sows discord among brethren.

What time is it?

It's time to declare War on the Devil!!!!

I read the end of the Bible. We Win!!! We Win!!We Win!!! No weapon formed against us shall prosper!!!

The Battle is not yours It's the LORD'S!!!!! So THAT'S WHAT TIME IT IS!!!!!!!!

LORD YOU ARE GOOD

You're a Good Father and I'm love by you. It is a pleasure to serve you. You have never let me down My life is dedicated to you. What would you have for me to do for you today? Just for waking me up this morning is more than I could ever ask for. Thank You Lord Jesus!! You are wonderful, Awesome, Faithful, True to Your Word, everything I need is in you. I can't live I can't move without you. You're the very breath I breathe. Guide me this day in your perfect will. I want you to be always on my mind. You are the first one I talk to in the morning and the last one I talk to ever night. What a Glorious Relationship we have!

Sincerely Your Daughter

Father God,

Thank You for waking me up this morning in my right mind.

Thank You for the moving and activity of my limbs I live and move and have my being in you. Now as I go through this day I pray for your angels around my vehicle, and you give me traveling mercy. I pray over my children, and family.

My Church Family and everyone that concerns me, for their safety. Thank You for the many blessings you have given me. May I be a blessing to somebody today.

In that I give you praise, honor and glory. In Jesus name, Amen.

GOOD MORNING LORD

Good Morning Lord, When I slumber and slept my sleep was sweet.

You are a good God and "I WOULD TRADE NOTHING FOR MY JOURNEY" with you. My Soul Magnify you, you are a present help in every way. I want to be a vessel humble and submitted to be used by you on a daily basis.

If I have sinned anyway against you In thought, action or word I repent. I want to die out of this flesh and walk in the Spirit. Please have mercy on me. I turn to your righteousness and goodness in obedience, that your favor may be continually in my life. Keep me in your loving arms that I may be safe to do your will. In that I give you Glory In Jesus name, . . .

                                                        Amen, amen!

ˈTHE GREAT PHYSICIAN

KING OF KINGS........LORD OF LORDS......ALPHA AND OMEGA.....THE BEGINNING AND THE END......THE ALMIGHTY.......THE FIRST AND THE LAST......THE ROOT AND THE OFFSPRING OF DAVID.....THE BRIGHT AND MORNING STAR....THE SON OF MAN......THE LORD OF THE SABBATH......KING OF THE JEWS......THE CHRIST, THE SON OF THE LIVING GOD.......A PROPHET......THE BRIDEGROOM......THE GREAT PHYSICIAN.......THE CHIEF CONORSTONE .... THE GOD OF ABRAMHAM, THE GOD ISAAC, AND THE GOD OF JACOB..... I AM .... WONDERFUL ...... COUNSELOR.....

MIGHTY GOD.....EVERLASTING FATHER.....

PRINCE OF PEACE......AMEN AMEN!!!!!!

REPENT AND PROSPER

Job 22:21-30

> [21] "Now acquaint yourself with him and be at peace, Therefore good will come to you.
>
> [22] Receive, please instruction from his mouth, And lay up his Words in your heart.
>
> [23] If you return to the Almighty, you will be built up; You will remove iniquity far from your tents.
>
> [24] Then you will lay your gold in the dust, And the gold of Ophir among the stones of the brooks.
>
> [25] Yes the Almighty will be your gold And your precious silver;
>
> [26] For then you will have your delight in the Almighty, And lift up your face to God.
>
> [27] You will make your prayer to Him, and He will hear you; And you will pay your vows.
>
> [28] You will also declare a thing, And it will be established for you; so light will shine on your ways.

> [29] When they cast you down and you say, 'Exaltation will come!' Then He will save the humble person.

> [30] He will even deliver one who is not innocent; Yes, He will be delivered by the purity of your hands."

There are 15 will's in these verses, That lets you know God has a will for our lives.

So If you Repent from any Sin you are doing and turn to God you will Prosper, Spiritually, Physically and Financially.

Don't you want to be Blessed by the best "Jesus"!!!!

Repent and Prosper

2 Chronicles 7:14 "if My people who are called by my name will humble themselves and pray and seek My face and turn from their wicked ways, then I will hear from heaven and forgive their sin and heal their land."

Repent and Prosper

Isaiah 65:23,24

> [23] They shall not labor in vain, Nor bring forth children for trouble; For they shall be the descendants of the blessed of the Lord, And their offspring with them.

> ²⁴ It shall come to pass that before they call, I will answer; and while they are still speaking I will hear.

Repent and Prosper

Proverbs 3:32,33

> ³² For the perverse person is an abomination to the Lord, But His secret counsel is with the upright.
>
> ³³ The curse of the Lord is on the house of the wicked, but He blesses the home of the just.

Act 2:38

> ³⁸ Then Peter said to him "Repent and let every one of you be baptized in the name of Jesus Christ for the remission of sins; and you shall receive the gift of the Holy Spirit.

Repent and Prosper

James 5: 15, 16

> ¹⁵ And the prayer of faith will save the sick, and the Lord will raise him up, And if he has committed sins, he will be forgiven.
>
> ¹⁶ Confess your trespasses to one another and pray for one another that you may be healed.

The effective, fervent prayer of a righteous man avails much.

Repent and Prosper

James 5: 19, 20

> [19] Brethren, if anyone among you wanders from the truth, and someone turns him back,
>
> [20] Let him know that he who turns a sinner from the error of his way will save a soul from death and cover a multitude of sins.

Repent and Prosper

Repent, you won't Lose your Song!

Repent, he'll let you know he Got You!

Repent, he Redeem you out the hands of the enemy
Repent, you will be forgiven

Repent, Jesus will change you

Repent, He'll put His Spirit in you and cause you to walk in his ways

Who Jesus! Who Jesus!

Numbers 23: 19,20

> [19] "God is not a man, that He should lie, Nor a son of man, that He should repent.

Has He said, and will He not do? Or has He spoken, and will he not make it good?

[20] Behold, I have received a command to bless; He has blessed and I cannot reverse it.

REPENT AND PROSPER!!!   REPENT AND PROSPER!!!!
REPENT AND PROSPER!!!!!!

DON'T LOSE YOUR SONG

Go to Acts 16:22-31 this is where this text is coming from.

Can you keep a song in your mouth through storms in your life? Will the devil get puzzled and say what can I do to them, they keep singing. Will he say let me find someone else to pick on! They're not afraid of me, just image you have been beaten and you still have a song in your heart.

Paul was a Pro in dealing with tough times and he gloried in tribulation

He was attacked time and time again, but he was sold out to Christ!

Philippians 4:13

> [13] I can do all things through Christ who strengthens me.

> *Don't Lose Your Song*

In James 1: 2-4

> [2] My brethren, Count it all joy when you fall into various trials,

³ Knowing that testing of your faith produces patience'

⁴ But let patience have its perfect work, that you may be perfect and complete, lacking nothing.

Paul was bold for Christ in Acts 13; 46, In Acts 14: 19 Paul had been stoned dragged out of the city supposing him to be dead.

So these are the things he went through for Christ sake, and The Church grew rapidly and increased daily.

Don't Lose Your Song

Your Church can grow too!! Stick to God 's Word and God's Word only. That's what Saved You from a burning Hell, it can save your whole family., And we could go on and on.

We are in the last days. Paul didn't let anyone come into his path without telling them about Jesus.

Who have you told about Jesus lately?

Colossians 3:16

Let the Word of Christ dwell in you richly in all wisdom teaching and admonishing one another in spiritual songs, singing with grace in your hearts to the Lord.

So don't lose your song. Even in Slave Days they sang ' Let my people Go'!

Don't Lose Your Song

As we had been Freed and Gospel songs inspired us and made us firm. Some music was:

"Hold On"....."Jesus Will Fix It" ......"Your Grace And Mercy"........"God Is A Good God"..."Precious Memories"...."Holy One"......"Never Could Have Made It"......We Love to Sing Your Praise....etc.

"Don't Lose Your Song "God gave you a voice he wants to hear it every day!!!!!!

Leviticus 23:40 They rejoice 7 days, that's everyday, Amen, amen.

YOU REAP WHAT YOU SOW

2 Corinthians 8:9

> ⁹ For you know the grace of our Lord Jesus Christ, that through he was rich, yet for your sake he became poor, so that you though his poverty might become rich.

2 Corinthians 9:6-12

> ⁶ But this I say: He who sows sparingly will also reap sparingly, and he who sows bountifully will also reap bountifully.

> ⁷ So let each one give as he purposes in his heart, not grudgingly or of necessity; for God loves a cheerful giver.

> ⁸ And God is able to make all grace abound toward you, that you, always having all sufficiency in all things, may have an abundance for every good work.

> ⁹ As it is written: He has dispersed abroad, He has given to the poor; His righteousness endures forever.

¹⁰ Now may He who supplies seed to the sower; and bread for food, supply and multiply the seed you have sown and increase the fruits of your righteousness,

¹¹ while you are enriched in everything for all liberality, which cause thanksgiving through us to God.

¹² For the administration of this service not only supplies the needs of the saints, but also is abounding through many thanksgivings to God.

If you were ever doing wisely with your money that you gather you will have no lack. Why would God say give your first fruits of your labor to Him, if he didn't have a plan to Bless you. God wants the best for you!

John 10-10

10) "The thief does not come except to steal, and to kill, and to destroy. I have come that they may have life, and that they may have it more abundantly."

In Genesis 14:20 Abram paid tithe to the High Priest Melchizedek. What's stored up in your heavenly treasure? Have you given enough Prayer Time, Praise Time, Worship Time, and Offering, have you given to the poor? Have you offered a meal to somebody.? Have you sowed a seed to any one that's not your family member or friend?

You Reap What You Sow!!!!

Job 36:11

11) If they obey and serve me (the Lord) you will spend your days in prosperity and your years in pleasure.

Proverbs 8:21

21) That I may cause those who love me to inherit wealth. That I may fill their treasures.

Proverbs 10-22

22) The blessings of the Lord makes one rich and adds no sorrow with it.

Isaiah 48:17

17) Thus says the Lord, your Redeemer, The Holy One of Israel: I am the Lord your God, Who teaches you to profit, Who leads you by the way you should go.

I don't know about you but I would rather be two steps behind God than one step in front of Him. I spent over half of my life leading myself. And it got me nowhere good. I was an accident going somewhere to happen. The Word of God will stop us from repeating our mistakes! Change your way of thinking.

You Reap What You Sow

There was a Women on her last meal with her Son. And the Man of God told her to bake his cake first and her meal barrel never ran out. Obedience is better than sacrifice.

You Reap What You Sow

So Say This:

I'm Healthy, Wealthy and Wise!!

I'm Prosperous!!

I'm a King's Kid!!

I'm not in Lack!!

I'm not Defeated!!

He always causes me to triumph!!

I'm more than a conqueror!!

I'm the head not the tail!!

I'm above only and not beneath!!

I'm the lender not the borrower!!

MY Reaping is going to overpower my sowing!!

You Reap What You Sow

                Amen, amen!!!!!!

LABOR OF LOVE PRAYER

Lord, by your stripes we are healed. You said the harvest is plentiful and the Labors are few, Pray that the Lord send labors into the harvest. God we need your spirit of laboring in your vineyard. You said make disciples until you come back. God you have not given us the Spirit of fear but of power and of love and a sound mind. You gave your life to redeem us back to you. Thank You! Let us be ready and willing to do as you ask us to for your glory. Enlighten our eyes to keep them steadfast on you. Let us not lean to our own understanding in all our ways acknowledge you and you shall direct our path. We are the head and not the tail. We are blessed in the city blessed in the field. Eyes have not seen ears have not heard nor has it enter into the heart of man what God has prepared for those who love him. We receive your Word because it will not come back void to you. We are made in your image so as You speak so can we speak and It will come to pass. God is not a man that he should lie; neither the son of man, that he should repent; has he said, will he not do? Or has he spoken, and shall he not make it good? We believe your Word, We stand on your Word We honor your Word! We give you all the Glory in Your Precious Son's

Name Jesus Christ our Lord and Savior Amen amen!!

I'M CHOSEN

Acts 9:10-18

¹⁰ Now there was a certain disciple at Damascus named Ananias; and to him the Lord said in a vision, "Ananias" And he said "Here I am Lord".

¹¹ So the Lord said to him, "Arise and go to street called Straight and inquire at the house of Judas for one called Saul of Tarsus for behold he is praying.

¹² And in a vision he has seen a man named Ananias coming in and putting his hand on him so that he might receive his sight."

¹³ Then Ananias answered, "Lord I have heard from many about this man; how much harm he has done to Your saints in Jerusalem."

¹⁴ And here he has authority from the chief priests to bind all who call Your name."

¹⁵ But the Lord said to him, "Go, for he is a chosen vessel of Mine to bear My name before Gentiles, Kings, and the Children of Israel.

> ¹⁶ For I will show how many things he must suffer for My name's sake.

> ¹⁷ And Ananias went his way and entered the house; and laying his hands on him he said, "Brother Saul, the Lord Jesus, who appeared to you on the road as you came has sent me that you may receive your sight and be filled with the Holy Spirit".

> ¹⁸ Immediately there fell from his eyes something like scales, and he received his sight at once; and he arose and was baptized.

Matthew 22:14

> ¹⁴ "For many are called, but few are chosen".

God has chosen many churches to birth common people that end up being great leaders all over the World. Some have even turned out to be Bishop's, Singers, and great leaders for the up- building of Gods Kingdom.

So Are You A Chosen Vessel?

2 Corinthians 4: 7-10

> ⁷ But we have this treasure in earthen vessels, that the excellence of the power may be of God and not us.

> ⁸ We are hard-pressed on every side, yet not crushed; we are perplexed, but not in despair;

⁹ persecuted, but not forsaken; struck down, but not destroyed-

¹⁰ always carrying about in the body the dying of the Lord Jesus, that the life of Jesus also may be manifested in our body.

So Are You A Chosen Vessel?

Choose Ye this Day Who You will Serve!!!!!!

Romans 8: 35-39

³⁵ Who shall separate us from the Love of Christ. Shall tribulation or distress or persecution, or famine, or nakedness or peril or sword?

³⁶ As it is written: For Your sake we are killed all day long; We are accounted as sheep for the slaughter.

³⁷ Yet in all these things we are more than conquerors through Him who loved us.

³⁸ For I am persuaded that neither death nor life, nor angels nor principalities nor powers, nor things present nor things to come,

³⁹ nor height nor depth, nor any other created thing, shall be able to separate us from the love of God which is in Christ Jesus our Lord.

To be chosen you must suffer with the Lord to also reign with him. What we go through is nothing compared of what he went through to redeem us from a burning Hell. Please forgive us God for complaining if we are misunderstood. Our service is the least that we can do for Him. Don't you agree?

Paul had been through many suffering until he called it light affliction. There was nothing to shake Paul's faith in Jesus.

"ARE YOU LIKE THAT" OR HEADED THAT WAY?"

Jesus was chosen before the foundation of the world to redeem man back to God.

Philippians 2:6-8

> 6 Who being in the form of God thought it not robbery to be equal with God.
>
> 7 But made himself of no reputation taking the form of a bond servant, and coming in the likeness of men.
>
> 8 And being found in appearance as a man, he humbled himself and became obedient to the point of death, even the death of the cross.

So once again I Ask, *"Are you A Chosen Vessel?"*

Can't Nobody Do You Like Jesus!!! Can't Nobody Keep You Like Jesus!!! NOBODY, NOBODY I MEAN NOBODY!!!!!! AMEN! AMEN!

HELL WAS NOT MADE FOR YOU

John 5:24- 30

²⁴ "Most assuredly, I say to you, he who hears My word and believes in him who sent me has everlasting life, and shall not come into judgment but has passed from death into life."

²⁵ "Most assuredly, I say to you, the hour is coming and now is, when the dead will hear the voice of the Son of God; and those who hear will live."

²⁶ For as the Father has life in himself, So He has granted the Son to have life in himself,

²⁷ and has given Him authority to execute judgment also, because He is the Son of Man.

²⁸ Do not marvel at this; for the hour is coming in which all who are in the graves will hear His voice

²⁹ and come forth-those who have done good, to the resurrection of life, and those who have done evil, to the resurrection of condemnation.

> [30] I can of Myself do nothing; As I hear, I judge, and My judgment is righteous because I do not seek My own will but the will of the Father who sent me.

The Bible tells us to work while it is day. The hour is coming when no man can work. When Jesus was on the cross, died, rose again, Went back home to heaven, sat down at the right hand of God. And now interceding for us, we pick up our cross and walk in the image of him now. And when he rose he rose for us to be saved by grace. Isn't that a wonderful thing!!!!!!!

Hell was not Made For You

2 Peter 2:4

> [4] For God did not spare the angels who sinned but cast them down to hell and delivered them into chains of darkness to be reserved for judgment.

Hell was not made for you!!!!! Hell was made for the Devil and his Angels!!! And if you go there that was not God's plan. The choice is yours, salvation is a free gift.

2 Peter 3:8,9

> [8] "But beloved, do not forget this one thing, that with the Lord one day is as a thousand years. And a thousand years as one day."
>
> [9] The Lord is not slack concerning His promises as some count slackness, but is long-suffering toward

us, not willing any should perish but that (all) should come to repentance.

God said: I Put My Spirit In You to Cause You To Walk In My Ways!!!

Galatians 5: 22, 23

> [22] But the fruit of the Spirit is Love, joy, peace, long-suffering, kindness, goodness, faithfulness,

> [23] gentleness self-control Against such there is no law.

No one comes to the Father except by me (Jesus). Every knee shall bow and every tongue shall confess that Jesus is Lord.

HELL Was Not Made For You

John 14: 1-3

Let not your heart be trouble; you believe in God believe also in me.

2) In My Father's house are many mansions. If it were not so I would have told you. I go to prepare a place for you.

3) And if I go and prepare a place for you I will receive you to Myself, that where I am, there you may be also.

HELL WAS NOT MADE FOR YOU!

DEATH, BURIAL, AND RESURRECTION!

EVERYTHING LEADS TO THE CROSS, BUT IT DIDN'T END THERE, He Got UP!!! And He's coming Back Again!!!!!!!!! Come Lord Jesus Come!!!

1 Thessalonians 4: 13-18

> [13] But I do not want you to be ignorant, brethren, concerning those who have fallen asleep, lest you sorrow as others who have no hope.
>
> [14] For if we believe that Jesus died and rose again, even so God will bring with him those who sleep in Jesus.
>
> [15] For this we say to you by the word of the Lord, that we who are alive and remain until the coming of the Lord will by no means precede those who are asleep.
>
> [16] For the Lord Himself will descend from heaven with a shout with the voice of an archangel, and with the trumpet of God. And the dead in Christ will rise first.
>
> [17] Then we are alive and remain shall be caught up together with them in the clouds to meet the Lord in the air. And thus we shall always be with the Lord.

[18] Therefore comfort one another with these words,

Hell Was Not Made For You

John 3: 16, 17

[16] For God so love the world that He gave His only begotten Son, that whosoever believes in him should not perish but have everlasting life.

[17] For God did not send his Son into the world to condemn the world but that the world through him might be saved.

HELL WAS NOT MADE FOR YOU!

Who the Son set Free is FREE INDEED!!!!!

Amen, amen

MY PRAYERS MAKES A DIFFERENCE

Lord when I look to the hills from which comes my help all my help comes from you. I'm so glad you made me the head and not the tail above only and not beneath. Thank You for love that's is unconditional. Out of all I've been through you never left me or forsaken me. I'm learning to be pleased with my relationship with You being my Maker and Husband. Lord you made a difference in my life when I felt there was no hope for me. When mountains seem to high you said I could climb them. Just lean not to my own understanding in all my ways acknowledge you and you shall direct my path. Thank you there is no fault you can't forgive, We have all fallen short of the glory because All the glory belong to you. I'm pouring my heart to you because you're the best thing that has ever happen to me. I needed forgiveness out of all the mistakes in my life. Sin is not my friend.!!! When I was at my lowest you brought me out of the miry clay, You got me from the gates of Hell. Just Thank You once again. Amen amen.....

PRAYERS CHANGES THINGS

There has never been a better time to pray than now in these last days. As a Matter of fact time is speeding up it's later than you think. The Bible is being more and more fulfilled right before our eyes.

2 Chronicles 7:14

> [14] "If My People who are called by my name will humble themselves and pray and seek My face and turn from their wicked ways then I will hear from heaven, and will forgive their sins and heal their land."

Judgment is going to begin in the house of God. We are the ones God is coming to first. And if we just scarcely make it in, What will it be for the unrighteous?

Psalm 66: 18- 20

> [18] If I regard iniquity in my heart The Lord will not hear (me)

> [19] But certainly God has heard me; He has attended to the voice of my prayer.

> [20] Blessed be God, Who has not turned away my prayer, Nor His mercy from me!

His mercy is new every morning,

Psalm 88:13

> [13] But to You I have cried out O Lord and in the morning my prayer comes before You.

Prayer Changes Things

Psalm 55: 17

> [17] Evening and morning and at noon I will pray, and cry aloud, And He shall hear my voice.

Psalm 5: 1-3

> [1] Give ear to my words, O Lord Consider my meditation.
>
> [2] Give heed to the voice of my cry, My King and my God, For to You I will pray.
>
> [3] My voice You shall hear in the morning, O Lord; In the morning I will direct it to You, And I will look up.

Paul prayed for God to take away this thorn out of his flesh, God said: My grace is sufficient for you.

Joshua prayed Let the Sun stand still until the battle was won with the Amorites and it was granted.

Jabez prayed for God to bless him and Enlarge his Territory and keep him from evil, that he may not cause pain.

Samson prayed that God would give him strength one more time to take vengeance on the Philistines.

Abraham prayed for Sodom and Gomorrah down to 10 people to save the city and God heard him.

Hannah prayed for a male child and God answered her prayer.

Hezekiah prayed for God to let him live and God gave him 15 more years'

Job prayed for his friends and God gave him double of all he had lost from Satan.

And What have you prayed about and God blessed you with an answer?

Prayer Changes Things

But Do You Want To Hear The Most Powerful Prayer of All By Jesus?

John Chapter 17: 1-5 for himself, John 17: 6-19 for his disciples, John 17: 20-26 for all believers

John 17: 20-26 says:

> [20] "I do not pray for these alone, but also for those who will believe in Me through their word.

[21] that they all may be one, as You, Father, are in Me, and I in You; that they also may be one in Us, that the world may believe that You sent me.

[22] And the glory which You gave Me I have given them, that they be one just as We are one:

[23] I in them, and You in Me; that they may be perfect in one, and that the world may know that You have sent Me, and have loved them as you have loved Me.

[24] Father; I desire that they also whom You gave Me may be with Me where I am; that they may behold My glory which You have given Me; for You loved Me before the foundation of the world.

[25] O Righteous Father! The world has not known You, but I have known You; and these have known that You sent Me.

[26] And I have declared to them Your name, and will declare it, that the love with which You loved Me may be in them, and I in them."

That's the Holy Ghost, The Holy Spirit which cause us to walk in God's ways!!!!!

Prayer Changes Things

Jesus Cleaned the Temple in Mark 11:17

Then He taught, saying to them, "Is it not written, 'My house shall be called a house of prayer for all nations? But you have made it a 'den of thieves.'"

REPENT PRAYER CHANGES THINGS........FORGIVE AND BE FORGIVEN

1) The disciples prayed for boldness

2) Stephen prayed "Lord charge not this sin against them".

3) Cornelius prayed always to God

4) Elijah prayed for it not to rain 3 and 1 half years, then prayed for it to rain and God answer him.

And the Model Prayer is Matthew 6: 9-13

[9] Our Father in heaven, Hallowed be your name.

[10] Your kingdom come. Your will be done On earth as it is in heaven.

[11] Give us this day our daily bread.

[12] And forgive us our debts, As we forgive our debtors.

[13] And do not lead us into temptation, But deliver us from evil.

For Yours is the kingdom and the power and the glory forever. Amen

Prayer Changes Things

Who Do You Call When You're in Trouble?

Some call him Wonderful

Some call him Counselor,

Some call him Mighty God,

Some call him Prince of Peace,

Some call him Healer,

Some call him Deliver.

Some call him a Lawyer in the Court Room,

Some call him Son of David

I call him JESUS.........He's my bread when I'm hungry........He's my Water when I'm thirsty.....

He shall supply all my need according to his riches and glory!!!!!!

Just Keep Praying Saints!!!! Truly he is the answer to all our prayers!!!!!

PRAYER CHANGES THINGS IT'S OUR ONLY COMMCATION WITH GOD..........AMEN AMEN!!!!!!

VIRTUOUS WOMAN

Sub Topic: Glad to be me!!!

Proverbs 31: 10

> [10] Who can find a virtuous woman? For her price is far above rubies.

Virtuous means 1) morally good 2) effective or commendable quality 3) chase

Moral means conforming to a standard of right behavior.

So this is a woman firm steadfast unshakeable in her ways of life. Also being planted in Holy Living!

And we say ladies: Glad to be me!!!

THIS Woman is Wife Material!!!

Faithful to the bone!!!!

She's ready for her Boaz to come into her life!!!

And we ladies say: Glad to be me!!!

The only other time virtuous woman is mention in the Bible was in Ruth 3:11

> [11] And now my daughter fear not; I will do to you all that you request for all the people of my town know that you are a virtuous woman.

Are there any virtuous women here?

To dress the part that would makes you attractive to Godly Men.

The way you dress makes a difference who comes to you! And where you go makes a difference who comes after you! As a Woman today some old school ways are still up to date believe it or not!!

Proverbs 18: 22

> [22] He who finds a wife, He who finds a wife, Finds a good thing, And obtains favor from the Lord!!

V= Victorious

I= integrity

R= right-standing

T= truthful

U= unforgettable

O= observant

U= understanding

S= sacred

And the ladies say: Glad to be me!!!

W= WEALTHY

O=OVERJOYED

M= MIRTH

A=ALERT

N=NOURISHING

Proverbs 31:10- 31

> [10] Who can find a virtuous woman? For her worth is far above rubies.
>
> [11] The heart of her husband safely trusts her; So he have no lack of gain.
>
> [12] She does him good and not evil All the days of her life.
>
> [13] She seeks wool and flax, And willingly works with her hands.
>
> [14] She is like the merchant ships, She brings her food from afar.

¹⁵ She also rises while it is yet night, And provides food for her household and a portion for her maidservants.

¹⁶ She considers a field and buys it; From her profits she plants a vineyard.

¹⁷ She girds herself with strength, And strengthens her arms.

¹⁸ She perceives that her merchandise is good, And her lamp does not go out by night.

¹⁹ She stretches out her hands to the distaff, And her hand holds the spindle.

²⁰ She extends her hand to the poor, Yes, she reaches out her hands to the needy.

²¹ She is not afraid of snow for her household, For all her household is clothes with scarlet.

²² She makes tapestry for herself; Her clothing is fine linen and purple.

²³ Her husband is known in the gates, When he sits among the elders of the land.

²⁴ She makes linen garments and sells them, And supplies sashes for the merchants.

²⁵ Strength and honor are her clothing; She shall rejoice in time to come.

²⁶ She opens her mouth with wisdom, And on her tongue is the law of kindness.

²⁷ She watches over the ways of her household, And does not eat the bread of idleness.

²⁸ Her children rise up and call her blessed, Her husband also, and he praises her:

²⁹ "Many daughters have done well, But you excel them all."

³⁰ Charm is deceitful and beauty is passing, But a woman who fears the Lord, she shall be praised.

³¹ Give her of the fruit of her hands, And let her own works praise her in the gates.

When the word talks about wisdom it is called her and she!!

And the ladies say: Glad to be me!!

Proverbs 3: 14-18

¹⁴ For her proceeds are better than the profits of silver.

¹⁵ She is more precious than rubies, And all the things you desire cannot compare with her.

> [16] Length of days is in her right hand, In her left riches and honor.
>
> [17] Her way are ways of pleasantness, And all her paths are peace.
>
> [18] She is a tree of life to those who take hold of her, And happy are all who retain her.

You say ladies: Glad to be me!!

"I am a Virtuous Woman."

We as women sometimes wear many hats to deal with life's ups and downs. This woman cared about her family, the poor, her maidservants, buying and selling. Nobody went without. She was also making her clothes. That's a woman a husband would be proud of. The Bible says the older women are suppose to train the younger women. To teach them how to be good mothers and wives!

Isaiah 54:5

> [5] For your maker is your husband, The Lord of hosts is his name; And your redeemer is the Holy One of Israel; He is called the God of the whole earth.

Glad to be me= I am the head and not the tail!!

Glad to be me= I am the loaner not the borrowed!!

Glad to be me= I am the righteousness of God because of Jesus!!

Glad to be me= I am blessed in the city and bless in the field!!

WE ARE THE VIRTUOUS WOMEN..............AMEN AMEN!!!!!!

FROM THE CURSE TO GRACE

1 Corinthians 9: 19-23

> ¹⁹ For through I am free from all men, I have made myself a servant, to all that I might win the more,

> ²⁰ And to the Jews I became as a Jew, that I might win Jews; to those who are under the law, as under the law; that I might win those who are under the law.

> ²¹ to those who are without law, as without law (not being without law toward God but under law toward Christ) that I might win those who are without.

> ²² to the weak I became a weak that I might win the weak. I have become all things to all men, that I might by all means save some.

> ²³ Now this I do for the gospel's sake, that I may be partaker of it with you.

The curse that was once on your life has been lifted off you because of the Blood of Jesus Christ. The

Anointing Destroyed The Yoke. Thank God for Jesus!! The Blood, that purchased our Salvation!

So Paul became all things to all people. Jesus did the same and Paul walked in that example.

Psalm 18: 43, 44

[43] You, have delivered me from the striving of people; You have made me the head of the nation; The people I have not known shall serve me.

[44] As soon as they hear of me they obey me; The foreigners submit to me.

From The Curse to Grace

1 Corinthians 15: 55-58

[55] "O Death where is your sting?"

O Hades, where is your victory?"

[56] The sting of death is sin, and the strength of sin is the law.

[57] But thanks be to God, who gives us the victory through our Lord Jesus Christ.

[58] Therefore, my beloved brethren, be steadfast, immoveable, always abounding in the work of the

Lord, knowing that your labor is not in vain in the Lord.

This is the last enemy "Death!" It has no power over our Lord Jesus! He is the last Adam. The first Adam was flesh. The second Adam was Spirit. Winning Souls is our daily task now. Talking about Jesus everywhere we go! God is not a hard taskmaster. His yoke is easy and his burden is light. We go through a light affliction.

From the Curse to Grace

So let us run this race to thee end, so we can see our Maker face to face in peace.

Ecclesiastes 12: 13, 14

> [13] Let us hear the conclusion of the whole matter: Fear God and keep His commandments, For this is man's all.
>
> [14] For God will bring every work into judgment, Including every secret thing. Whether good or evil.

How much time of your life have you devoted to helping someone else, someone on your job, in the store, at the cleaners. Do you say to a stranger standing around a business door asking for money (change), I don't have it I gave to somebody else. That's your neighbor. The poor we will have with us always! Give and it will be given unto you good measure, press down shaken together, and running over will men give unto your blossom. All Glory To God!

Nadine V. Hadley

From the Curse to Grace

Proverbs 11: 30

> [30] The fruit of the righteous is a tree of life, And he who wins souls is wise.

Proverbs 11: 25

> [25] The generous soul will be made rich, And he who waters will also be watered himself.

God's Business is the biggest business on earth. Only What You Do For Christ Will Last!!!

We went From the Curse to Grace! UNMERITED FAVOR! We got what we didn't deserve!!

AND I SAY AGAIN AND AGAIN FROM THE CURSE TO GRACE AMEN AMEN!!!

THANK YOU JESUS

Thank You Jesus for waking me up in my right mind. Thank You for the moving and active of my limbs. Thank you for the Blood still running warm in my veins. For this is the day that the Lord has made and I will rejoice and be glad in it. Any way you bless me I'll be satisfied. I appreciated where I am in life because I could have been in a Nation with no water, no food. May I be a blessing to those people in that state by giving money and prayer. Lord you are so good and your mercy is forever. I bless your name. Worthy is the Lamb that was slain before the foundation of the world. It is a blessing to be saved in these last days. Thank God we know you are coming back for a church without a spot or wrinkle. Thank You for the Blood of Jesus that purchased our Salvation. Thank you for who you are and what you have done on the cross.

You paid the price for my life, that cost more than silver and gold. You shed your Blood on Calvary. On that I praise you as long as I live.

HALLELUJAH IN JESUS NAME AMEN!!!!!

YOUR FAITH MAKES YOU PRAISE

Hebrews 11: 1-3

> 1 Now faith is the substance of things hoped for, the evidence of things not seen.
>
> 2 For by it the elders obtained a good testimony.
>
> 3 By faith we understand that the worlds were framed by the word of God, so that things which are seen were not made of things which are visible.

When you have faith, in every area in your life, Faith makes you praise God of how he brought you through your storms, strongholds, trials, tests, hard times, and difficult times. You get build up when you past the test. That lets you know, I had to step out on faith and God came through for me. Faith Moves God!!!

Luke 10: 17-20

> 17 Then the seventy returned with joy, saying, "Lord even the demons are subject to us in Your name."
>
> 18 And He said to them, "I saw Satan fall like lightning from heaven."

¹⁹ Behold, I give you the authority to trample on serpents and scorpions, and over all the power of the enemy, and nothing shall by any means hurt you.

²⁰ Nevertheless do not rejoice in this, that the spirits are subject to you, but rather rejoice because your names are written in heaven."

Luke 13: 10-13

¹⁰ Now He was teaching in one of the synagogues on the Sabbath.

¹¹ And behold, there was a woman who had a spirit of infirmity eighteen years, and was bent over and could in no way raise herself up.

¹² But when Jesus saw her, He called her to Him and said to her, "Woman, you are loosed from your infirmity."

¹³ And He laid His hands on her, and immediately she was made straight, and glorified God.

Her faith was, She kept coming to the temple and one day on the Sabbath it paid off, And she gave God the Praise.

Your Faith Makes You Praise

God was also always bringing David safely through attacks from his enemies. David kept a Praise on his lips!!

Psalm 92: 1,2

> [1] It is good to give thanks to the Lord, And to sing praises to Your name, O Most High;
>
> [2] To declare Your loving kindness in the morning, And Your faithfulness every night,

We as saints have a right and reason to praise God.

"If walls could talk,

"Hospital Rooms, and

"Nursing Homes

God came in and healed you. He visited us and recover us and gave sight to the blind.

Your Faith Makes You Praise

So many times I heard the Doctors say, "Those Church people get healed so fast and they don't stay sick long" And this is true, because we have someone we can call on, His name is Jesus!!

Psalm 89: 5

> [5] And the heaven will praise Your wonders, O Lord; Your faithfulness also in the assembly of the saints.

Your Faith Makes You Praise

Psalm 34: 1-3

> [1] I will bless the Lord at all times; His praise shall continually be in my mouth.
>
> [2] My soul shall make its boast in the Lord; The humble shall hear of it and be glad.
>
> [3] Oh magnify the Lord with me, And let us exalt His name together.

Your Faith Makes You Praise

Romans 12: 3

> [3] For I say, through the grace given to me, to everyone who is among you, not to think of himself more highly than he ought to think, but to think soberly, as God has dealt to each one a measure of faith.

Just think Joshua and Caleb had to wait 40 years to go into the Promise Land. Caleb had a different kind of spirit. He reminded Joshua God promised this land. He said "I'm just as strong now as I was back then."

Your Faith Makes You Praise

When we tear down every barrier of the enemy, We conqueror things that hold us back from reaching our destiny.

Tied up, Tangle, Lose Him, Lose Her, Lose Them. I don't believe he brought me this far to leave me!!! God said "He will never leave you nor forsake you."

You're on a mission! Are you going somewhere for God!! If God be for you who can be against you.

Your Faith Makes You Praise

Hebrews 11: 6

> [6] But without faith it is impossible to please Him, for he who comes to God must believe that He is, and that He is a rewarded of those who diligently see Him.

AND I WILL SAY IT TIME AND TIME AGAIN YOUR FAITH MAKES YOU PRAISE AMEN AMEN!!!!

SOME ONE'S KNOCKING AT THE DOOR

Luke 11: 5-9

> ⁵ And He said to them, "Which of you shall have a friend, and go to him at midnight and say to him, Friend, lend me three loaves;
>
> ⁶ for a friend of mine has come to me on his journey, and I have nothing to set before him;
>
> ⁷ and he will answer from within and say, 'Do not trouble me; the door is now shut, and my children are with me in bed; I cannot rise and give to you"?
>
> ⁸ I say to you, though he will not rise and give to him because he is his friend, yet because of his persistence he will rise and give him as many as he needs.
>
> ⁹ So I say to you, ask, and it will be given to you; seek, and you will find; knock, and it will be opened to you.

To walk this Word in the Bible you got to be like a sheep, lead by the Shepherd. How many times has God been knocking at the door of your heart, and you didn't let him in. There may come a time you call on him and he won't answer. In Noah days he was building and ark for 120 years. Noah told the people it was going to rain. Nobody believed him until it began to rain. God shut the door on the Ark 8 souls was saved and 1 male and female of each living thing was kept alive, From animals to creeping things.

John 10: 9

> [9] I am the door. If anyone enters by Me, he will be saved, and will go in and out and find pasture.

Some One's Knocking at the Door

Acts 12: 5-7 & 11-13, & 16

> [5] Peter was therefore kept in prison; but constant prayer was offered to God for him by the church.

> [6] And when Herod was about to bring him out, that night Peter was sleeping, bound with two chains between two soldiers; and the guards before the door were keeping the prison.

> [7] Now behold, an angel of the Lord stood by him, and a light shone in the prison; and he struck Peter on the side and raised him up, saying, "Arise quickly!" And his chains fell off his hands.

¹¹ And when Peter had come to himself, he said, "Now I know for certain that the Lord has sent His angel, and has delivered me from the hand of Herod and from all the expectation of the Jewish people."

¹² So, when he had considered this, he came to the house of Mary, the mother of John whose surname was Mark, where many were gathered together praying.

¹³ And as Peter knocked at the door of the gate, a girl named Rhoda came to answer.

¹⁶ Now Peter continued knocking; and when they opened and saw him they were astonished.

Peter's life was hanging in the balance from the Jews but God had another plan for his life. Don't you be afraid God has a plan for your life too! And it's good. Do you know where you're going? Answer the door. Time is winding up it's later than you think. It's getting late in the evening the Sun in going down. The clock is ticking you're not getting any younger. Jesus is at the door!

Some One's knocking at the Door

So What it's Summer! Do you go on a trip you are not prepared for? What would you trade your soul for? This train has a one way ticket! This train is bound for Glory. The only way you ride you got to be Holy!

Joshua says, "Choose you this day who you will serve."

Joseph says, How then can I do this great wickedness, and sin against God?"

David was a man after God's own heart.

Abraham trusted God enough to sacrifice his only son.

Paul was sold out ready to die for the gospel.

Peter thought himself not to be worthy put to crucified the same way as his Lord and chose crucifixion upside down.

John the Baptist was willing to decrease as Jesus increased.

What would you be willing to do for Christ? Only what you do for Christ will last.

Rev. 3: 20-22

> [20] Behold, I stand at the door and knock. If anyone hears My voice and opens the door, I will come in to him and dine with him, and he with Me.
>
> [21] To him who overcomes I will grant to sit with Me on My throne, as I also overcame and sat down with My Father on His throne.

[22] He who has an ear; let him hear what the Spirit says to the churches.

When we were born we were born in Sin and shaped in iniquity, But it don't have to end that way! You can have every lasting life! Today is the day of Salvation!

SOME ONE'S KNOCKING AT THE DOOR LET HIM IN, IT'S JESUS, YOU WANT REGET IT AMEN AMEN!!!!!!

IT CAME FROM YOUR WOMB

Genesis 30: 22-24

> [22] Then God remembered Rachel, and God listened to her and opened her womb.
>
> [23] And she conceived and bore a son, and said. "God has taken away my reproach."
>
> [24] So she called his name Joseph, and said, "The Lord shall add to me another son."

Esther 2:7

> [7] And Mordecai had brought up Hadassah, that is Esther, his uncle's daughter, for she had neither father nor mother. The young woman was lovely and beautiful. When her father and mother died, Mordecai took her as his own daughter.

Are you in labor? Are you pregnant with destiny? Are you about to give birth to some one that would change people's lives?

God is no respect of a person if he did anything once he can do it again.

In these two children that was just ordinary, The Lord made them stand out and be notice in spite of their present circumstances.

One is a dreamer with favor on his life. And then here is a young woman chosen to be a queen.

Do you really know what you are carrying? Whether it came from your womb or not, you were held by God to take care of that child. As a mother you become attached 9 months and a close encounter with that baby. As a father you train and mold, correct, and protect and speak into their lives. With Esther God had a ram in the bush. He promised he will never leave you nor forsake you.

Believe me the devil can only go so far then God will take that sorrow and turn it in to joy.

Psalm 30: 5,6

> [5] For His anger is but for a moment, His favor is for life; Weeping may endure for a night, But joy comes in the morning.
>
> [6] Now in my prosperity I said, "I shall never be moved."

Joseph had favor in every area of his life.

Psalm 71: 21

> [21] You shall increase my greatness, And comfort me on every side.

For seven years while Joseph was in second command there was plenty, and seven years later, there was famine. But Joseph was wise in saving a supply in abundance. His dreams came to pass.

Psalm 127: 3

> ³ Behold children are a heritage from the Lord, The fruit of the womb is a reward.

Psalm 115: 14

> ¹⁴ May the Lord give you increase more and more, You and your children.

Then we read about Esther a virgin raised by her uncle Mordecai a Jew. She was taken to the palace to be beautified in preparation to meet the king. Vashti refused to come at the king's command and brought his anger, making it a public disrespect to all men. So he made a decree that husbands are not to be refused by their wives, whether they be great or small.

Esther 2: 16,17

> ¹⁶ So Esther was taken to King Ahasuerus, into his royal palace, in the tenth month, which is the month of Tebeth, in the seventh year of his reign.

> ¹⁷ The king loved Esther more than all the other women, and she obtained grace and favor in his sight more than all the virgins; so he set the royal crown upon her head and made her queen instead of Vashti.

It Came From Your Womb

John 14: 12

> ¹² "Most assuredly, I say to you, he who believes in Me, the works that I do he will do also; because I go to My Father.

Today in some cases babies are more mature when born, and can see clearly sometimes right after birth. When they become toddlers they are interested in computers, internet, cellphones, e-mail. We are more advanced than the early Biblical days.

1 Timothy 4:12

> ¹² Let no one despise your youth, but be an example to the believers in word, in conduct, in love, in spirit, in faith in purity.

Ecclesiastes 12: 1

> ¹ Remember now your Creator in the days of your youth, Before the difficult days come, And the

years draw near when you say, "I have no pleasure in them".

Psalm 144: 12

[12] That our sons may be as plants grown up in their youth; That our daughters may be as pillars, Sculptured in palace style;

Though your beginning may be small, your latter may be great!

IT CAME FROM YOUR WOMB

AMEN, AMEN!

IT'S PRAYING TIME

Sub Topic: Much Prayer Much Powerful

Philippians 4: 3-7

> ³ And I urge you also, true companion, help these women who labored with me in the gospel, with Clement also and the rest of my fellow workers whose names are in the Book of Life.
>
> ⁴ Rejoice in the Lord always. Again I will say, rejoice!
>
> ⁵ Let your gentleness be known to all men. The Lord is at hand.
>
> ⁶ Be anxious for nothing, but in everything by prayer and supplication, with thanksgiving, let your requests be made known to God;
>
> ⁷ and the peace of God, which surpasses all understanding, will guard your hearts and minds through Christ Jesus.

There is Power in God's Word when you pray.

Philippians is Paul most warmly written personal letter. After initial differences in the city of Philippians a strong bond developed between Paul and the converts there. Paul wrote to thank the church for a gift they had recently sent him in prison and to inform them of his circumstances.

The text of this letter from Paul suggest several characters of the church at Philippians. First Gentiles dominated. Few Jews lived in Philippians, Second, women, had a significant role. Third the church was generous. Fourth, they remained deeply loyal to Paul.

Prayer can get to a situation quicker than you can. When trouble comes pray NOW not later! Call on the name of Jesus, He will answer! The prayer of the righteous avails much. Prayer changes things. Prayer stops the Devil right in his tracks! Prayer interceding on our behalf right now as we speak. Prayer stands in the gab even for your love ones and friends.

It's Praying Time (Much Prayer Much Power)

Esther prayed and fasted for three days and it saved her and her people. Chapter 4

Joshua prayed and the Sun stood still for a whole day until he won the battle with the Amorites. Chapter 10

Samson prayed that he may receive strength one more time to kill the Philistine his enemies. Judges 16.

Hezekiah prayed and was healed and the given 15 more years to live. Isaiah 38.

Solomon prayed and was the wises and riches king ever lived. I King 3.

Job prayed for his friends and God gave him double for all he had lost from Satan. Chapter 42.

It's Praying Time (Much Prayer Much Power)

And Since It's Praying Time, What are you Praying for?

The righteous cry and God hears and not only hear He answers!!!

Prayer was important to Paul and should always be the way to command each issue in our lives and show God we need Him. He loves to show up and show out. Nobody Greater, Nobody Wiser, Nobody stronger, than Our God. There is none who can compare to Gods wisdom.

It's Praying Time (Much Prayer Much Power)

Philippians 1: 3-6

> [3] I thank my God upon every remembrance of you,
>
> [4] always in every prayer of mine making request for you all with joy,
>
> [5] for the fellowship in the gospel from the first day until now,

⁶ being confident of this very thing, that He begun a good work in you will complete it until the day of Jesus Christ.

It's Praying Time (Much Prayer Much Power)

Colossians 1: 3

³ We give thanks to the God and Father of our Lord Jesus Christ, praying always for you,

It's Praying Time (Much Prayer Much Power)

Jesus prayed for himself in John Chapter 17: 1-5

Jesus prayed for his disciples in John Chapter 17: 6-19

Jesus prayed for all believers in John 17: 20-26

And if Jesus Prayed You know we got to Pray!!! IT'S PRAYING TIME, PRAY, PRAY, PRAY, AMEN AMEN!!!!

WHAT ARE YOU DOING WITH YOUR TIME? (SEEK HIM)

Matthew 6: 33

> ³³ But seek first the kingdom of God and His righteousness, and all these things shall be added to you.

First of all who do you spend most of your time with? Who can get your attention when trouble comes? Who do you call on a daily basis?

Proverbs 6: 30, 31

> ³⁰ People do not despise a thief If he steals to satisfy himself when he is starving.
>
> ³¹ Yet when he is found, he must restore sevenfold; He may have to give up all the substance of his house.

Do you know the Devil is still paying for what he did in the garden with Adam and Eve!!!!

John 10:10,11

> [10] The thief does not come except to steal, and kill, and to destroy. I have come that they may have life, and that they may have it more abundantly.
>
> [11] I am the good shepherd. The good shepherd gives His life the sheep.

What are you doing with your time? (SEEK HIM)

Psalm 1:2

> [2] But his delight is in the law of the Lord, And in his law he meditates day and night.

Spending time with the Word is the best medicine you can get not:

Advil....

Tylenol......

Bayer Aspirin.....

These are things for your head!!!!!! THE WORD OF GOD IS FOR YOUR ....

Joshua 1:8

> [8] This Book of the Law shall not depart from your mouth, but you shall meditate in it day and night, that you may observe to do according to all that is

written in it. For then you will make your way prosperous, and then you will have good success.

God's Book The Holy Bible has the Plan for your Life. Follow his instruction you won't go wrong!!!!!!

Isaiah 26:3

> ³ You will keep him in perfect peace, Whose mind is stayed on You, Because he trusts in You.

What are you doing with your time? (SEEK HIM)

We are still reaping the benefits that was done on Calvary. It can't get no better than that!!!

The Pure, Holy, Righteous, No Blemish Blood shed on the cross for your sins and mind has been purchase for our Salvation, Deliverance, Healing, Demon chasing out, Cancer Rebuking, Sugar Diabetes, Mind Regulator, Heart fixer, wash and cleanse from all unrighteousness.

Who wouldn't want to serve a God like this? "The fool has said in his heart there is no God." What more proof do you need? Jesus is Lord of All!! Have you given your life to Jesus?

What are you doing with your time? (SEEK HIM)

Jeremiah 29:11

> ¹¹ For I know the thoughts that I think toward you, thoughts of peace and not of evil, to give you a future and a hope.

What are doing with your time? (SEEK HIM)

Romans 1:16,17

16) For I am not ashamed of the gospel of Christ, for it is the power of God to salvation for everyone who believes, for the Jews first and also for the Greeks.

17) For in the righteousness of God is revealed from faith to faith; as it is written, "The just shall live by faith."

SPEND YOUR TIME WISELY. WHAT ARE YOU DOING WITH YOUR TIME (SEEK HIM) Amen!!!!!!

THERE IS A FINALLY

Philippians 4:8,9

> ⁸ Finally brethren, whatever things are true, whatever things are noble, whatever things are just, whatever things are pure, whatever things are lovely, whatever things are of good report, if there is any virtue and if there is anything praiseworthy- meditate on these things.
>
> ⁹ The things which you learned and received and heard and saw in me, these do and the God of peace will be with you.

There is things God ask us to do. The writer of this part of the Bible is Paul. Everybody has a Finally. What will your Finally be?

Finally we know this world is going to come to an end. We also know that those who remain saved will be caught up to meet the Lord in thee air and forever be with our Lord.

Philippians 3:1

> [1] Finally my brethren, rejoice in the Lord. For me to write the same things to you is not tedious, but for you it is safe.

There is a Finally

Paul could rejoice in the darndest places and in the most difficult times in his life. After being beaten, shipwreck, in jail, trial, let down in a basket to escape for his life, you name it he did it!!!

1 Thessalonians 4:1

> [1] Finally then, brethren, we urge and exhort in the Lord Jesus that you should abound more and more, just as you received from us how you ought to walk and please God;

Holiness is a life style after you have been saved. You got to maintain righteous living. After all the world is looking at you. You represent our Lord and Savior. It's a Worship Experience.

2 Thessalonians 3:1-3

> [1] Finally, brethren, pray for us, that the word of the Lord may run swiftly and be glorified, just as it is with you,
>
> [2] and that we be delivered from unreasonable and wicked men; for not all have faith.

> [3] But the Lord is faithful, who will establish you and guard you from the evil one.

There is a Finally

I'm so glad Satan is under my feet. I don't trust him behind my back. He just might want to whisper something in my ear!!! I want my hear what the Holy Spirit has to say only Amen!

Ephesians 6:10,11

> [10] Finally, my brethren, be strong in the Lord and in the power of His might.
>
> [11] Put on the whole armor of God, that you may be able to stand against the wiles of the devil.

I heard a Preacher say "Satan is an old man. He's been around a long time." But God has been around forever he has no aging. He's time out side of time. He's forever beyond forever. He knows every trick the Devil would think to deceive us.

Thank God for Jesus!! Thank God for sending his only begotten Son!!! The Death, Burial, and Resurrection...... It all leads to the Cross!!!!!! We are Blood Bought, that's final!!!!!

Ecclesiastes 7:8

> ⁷ The end of a thing is better than its beginning; The patient in spirit is better than the proud in spirit.

Don't be in such a hurry that you miss what God has for you. Good things come for those who wait on the Lord. Wait for your answered prayer. He has so much greater value if you hold on to him. Don't set your mind on earthly things there temporary. Eternal Life is forever!!!

THERE IS A FINALLY TO SEE OUR MAKER THE CREATOR OF ALL THINGS AMEN AMEN!!!!!

"I MADE IT"

Lord I give you honor and praise to have an opportunity to spread your Word to one end of the earth to the other. Your Word is a lamp to my feet, and a light to my path. You are amazing, You are and awesome God. No one worthy can compare to you! Thank You for putting your anointing on this Book. Let it be a blessing to all Preachers and Teachers male and female of your Word. This is your Word, We are your people let our heart be on one accord and that is to spread the gospel of Jesus Christ. Let more be saved than ever before from this tool of Sermons and Prayers. Let us be carriers your Word putting out the fire the Devil started and pulling Souls back to the Kingdom of God. Let this bring more family closer together, Churches and Homes. Thank you Lord for putting your Spirit in me and Being Confident of this very thing, He that began a good work in me shall complete it until the day of Jesus Christ. I Made It because of you Jesus, and no one get the credit but God for this project!!! And on that note I seal this with a Praise HALLELUJAH JESUS, AMEN!!!

www.ingramcontent.com/pod-product-compliance
Lightning Source LLC
Chambersburg PA
CBHW061458040426
42450CB00008B/1405